2017

S0-BBE-297

HOORAY FOR FARMERS!

by Kurt Waldendorf

BUMBA BOOKS™

LERNER PUBLICATIONS ◆ MINNEAPOLIS

Note to Educators:

Throughout this book, you'll find critical thinking questions. These can be used to engage young readers in thinking critically about the topic and in using the text and photos to do so.

Copyright © 2017 by Lerner Publishing Group, Inc.

All rights reserved. International copyright secured. No part of this book may be reproduced, stored in a retrieval system, or transmitted in any form or by any means—electronic, mechanical, photocopying, recording, or otherwise—without the prior written permission of Lerner Publishing Group, Inc., except for the inclusion of a brief quotation in an acknowledged review.

Lerner Publications Company
A division of Lerner Publishing Group, Inc.
241 First Avenue North
Minneapolis, MN 55401 USA

For reading levels and more information, look up this title at www.lernerbooks.com.

Library of Congress Cataloging-in-Publication Data

Names: Waldendorf, Kurt, author.
Title: Hooray for farmers! / by Kurt Waldendorf.
Other titles: Hooray for community helpers!
Description: Minneapolis : Lerner Publications, [2016] | Series: Bumba books— Hooray for
    community helpers! | Includes bibliographical references and index.
Identifiers: LCCN 2016001070 (print) | LCCN 2016002239 (ebook) | ISBN
    9781512414431 (lb : alk. paper) | ISBN 9781512414776 (pb : alk. paper) |
    ISBN 9781512414783 (eb pdf)
Subjects: LCSH: Farmers—Juvenile literature.
Classification: LCC S519 .W33 2016 (print) | LCC S519 (ebook) | DDC 630.92—dc23

LC record available at http://lccn.loc.gov/2016001070

Manufactured in the United States of America
1 – VP – 7/15/16

Expand learning beyond the printed book. Download free, complementary educational resources for this book from our website, www.lernerresource.com.

LERNER
SOURCE

Table of
Contents

Farmers

Farmers help plants and

animals grow.

They work on farms.

Farms use lots of land.
Farmers plant crops
on this land.
Animals live on the
land too.

Farmers use big machines.

This farmer pulls a plow

with a tractor.

The plow gets the ground ready

for seeds.

Why do you think farmers might need big machines?

Seeds grow into crops.
Corn grows high out of
the ground.
Farmers use a combine
to pick the corn.

Some farmers do not need machines.

This farmer uses her hands.

She collects chicken eggs.

Farmers take care of animals.

The animals grow from babies

to adults.

Farmers keep the animals healthy.

This farmer feeds a baby pig.

What other
ways do you
think farmers
care for
their animals?

Farmers provide the food we eat.

We eat eggs and meat from

chickens.

We eat the corn that grows

in fields.

What other foods do farmers grow?

Farmers know a lot about farm animals and crops.

They learn from other farmers.

Other people go to college to learn too.

Farming is hard work.

Farmers wake up early

to care for animals.

They work all day long.

Farmer Tools

plow

tractor

combine

seeds

Picture Glossary

collects

gathers or picks things

combine

a machine that collects crops

crops

plants grown for food or goods

plow

a machine that digs up soil

Index

Read More

Jeffries, Joyce. *Meet the Farmer*. New York: Gareth Stevens, 2014.

Meister, Cari. *Farmers*. Minneapolis: Bullfrog Books, 2015.

Siemens, Jared. *Farmer*. New York: AV2 by Weigl, 2015.

Photo Credits

The images in this book are used with the permission of: © emholk/iStock.com, p. 5; © MaxyM/ Shutterstock.com, pp. 6–7; © tanger/Shutterstock.com, pp. 9, 23 (bottom right); © Jan van Broekhoven/ Shutterstock.com, pp. 10–11, 23 (top right); © Phovoir/Shutterstock.com, pp. 12, 23 (top left); © andresr/ iStock.com, p. 15; © Monkey Business Images/Shutterstock.com, p. 16; © simonkr/iStock.com, p. 19; © Air Images/Shutterstock.com, pp. 20–21; © Charles Brutlag/Shutterstock.com, p. 22 (top); © stefan11/ Shutterstock.com, p. 22 (bottom right); © Ekaterina Lin/Shutterstock.com, p. 22 (bottom left); © Sea Wave/Shutterstock.com, p. 23 (bottom left).

Front Cover: © Alexander Raths/Shutterstock.com.